Dr Zardos and the Mind Stone

Written by Max Greenslade

Illustrated by Alex Stitt

Flying Start
to Literacy®

Dr Zardos

Contents

19 June, morning:
Secret agents' headquarters

Secret agents Roxby and Crispo had been called to a meeting with Inspector Morris.

"We need your help," said the inspector to Roxby and Crispo. "The evil Dr Zardos has found the long lost Mind Stone."

"Doesn't the Mind Stone have the power to control the minds of everyone on Earth?" asked Roxby.

"It does," said Inspector Morris.
"But it can only be made to work at
one time – midnight in three days.
Then Dr Zardos can use the Mind
Stone to make everyone his slaves."

"He must be stopped,"
said Crispo.

"But how?" asked Roxby.

"You need three things,"
said Inspector Morris. "But these
three things are hidden around
the world. You must use the clues
in this top secret document to find
these things and stop Dr Zardos."

"Don't worry," said Crispo.
"We're on the case."

Secret agents' airfield

"What is the first clue?" asked Crispo.

"I'll read it," said Roxby.

Find the biggest pyramid
in all the lands.
Bigger than those in
desert sands.
Climb and climb and
do not stop.
The Star of Hope is
at the top.

"I know where the pyramids are," said Crispo. "They're in the desert in Egypt!"

"But the clue says that the pyramid is bigger than those in desert sands," said Roxby.

Crispo checked the Internet. "There is a pyramid in Mexico," he said. "It's the biggest pyramid ever built."

Roxby and Crispo got in their jet and went to Mexico.

WHOOOOOSH!

20 June: Mexico

"Is this a pyramid?" said Crispo.
"It looks like a hill."

"Look more closely," said Roxby.
"It's an enormous pyramid covered
with dirt.   Let's start climbing.
It is a long way to the top."

Crispo and Roxby climbed and
climbed until they got to the
top of the pyramid.

"Look for a clue," said Roxby.

Crispo and Roxby looked everywhere.
Then Roxby saw a carving of a brain.

"That looks just like the Mind Stone,"
she said.

Roxby pushed the carving. There
was a grinding noise and a panel
slid open. Inside was the
Star of Hope.

"We've found it," said Roxby.
"Where to next?"

Roxby read the second clue.

The Rock of Truth
is under a stone.
The stone is a statue
that stands alone.
The stone is the heaviest
of them all.
1000 tonnes and
metres tall.

"Heavy stones were used to build temples," said Crispo, checking the Internet.

"But a temple is a building. We need to find a statue," said Roxby.

"There is a huge statue in Egypt that was carved from a huge stone," said Crispo. "And it weighs 1000 tonnes."

"That has to be it," said Roxby. "Let's go to Egypt."

And off they zoomed.

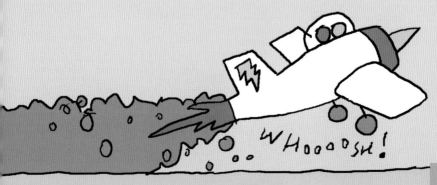

WHooooSH!

21 June: Egypt

"Look at that huge statue,"
said Roxby.

"If the Rock of Truth
is under the statue,
we'll have to dig it out,"
said Crispo.

"I don't think so," said Roxby.
"Look, there is another carving
of a brain."

Roxby pressed the carving and a
panel slid open.   And there
was the Rock of Truth.

"Two down, one to go!" said Crispo.
"Where to next?"

Roxby read the third clue.

The longest wall ever made,
Built with mud
and bricks well laid.
It kept out enemies
and kept in friends.
The Jewel of Love
is at the end.

"I think the longest wall is Hadrian's Wall," said Roxby.

"I'll check on the Internet," said Crispo. "No, Hadrian's Wall is only 70 kilometres long."

"Well, what is the longest wall?" said Roxby.

"It's the Great Wall of China," said Crispo. "It's more than 6700 kilometres long."

"Of course!" said Roxby.

They got in their jet and zoomed off to China.

22 June, midday: China

"Look at this wall," said Crispo.
"It goes for such a long way."

"We are nearly at the end," said
Roxby. "Look for a carving of
a brain."

"Look over there," said Crispo.
"I can see a carving of a brain."

Roxby and Crispo landed the jet.
When they touched the carving, a
panel slid open.

"Here it is," said Roxby. "We've
found the Jewel of Love. Quick, we
are running out of time. We must
stop Dr Zardos."

22 June, midnight: England

Dr Zardos held the Mind Stone high above his head.

"Now I will rule the world," he said.

"I don't think so," said Crispo as he held up the Star of Hope and the Rock of Truth.

"Ha! Ha!" laughed Dr Zardos. "You can't stop me! You don't have the Jewel of Love."

"Yes, we do," said Roxby, as she stepped out into the moonlight with the Jewel of Love.

"No! No! NO!" screamed Dr Zardos.

There was a flash of lightning and the Mind Stone shattered into a thousand pieces.

23

"That's the end of you, Dr Zardos," said Crispo.

"The world is now a safer place," said Roxby.

"Well done, Roxby and Crispo," said Inspector Morris. "You have saved the world once again!"